The back of each page has
reader's notes, comments, etc.

TEMPO … Heartbeat of the Golf Swing
The Little Blue Book I, copyright © 2009
By John Michael Saraceno, Golf Educator.

ISBN 978-1449536862

Notes:

Contents

Notes:

Dedication

She was a very good friend, confidant, and the best cook on the planet…….the only one that thought my getting involved in golf as a profession was a good idea. My mother, Josephine, you are loved and thought of often.

Notes:

A New Vista

There are 51 million golfers worldwide filling the golf courses and practice ranges diligently searching for a swing that will improve their golf game.

In my 20 years as a golf educator it has become evident to me that there is only one thing that can unite all the techniques involved in a swing. That one thing is TEMPO.

TEMPO is the heartbeat of the golf swing. In this "Little Blue Book I" you will find the missing link. With my formula you will be able to apply TEMPO consistently to your golf swing.

Good TEMPO will sharpen your mental focus, thereby, controlling your swing techniques. Utilizing this formula, you'll have the format to apply TEMPO to your swing which will improve your golf game.

End the frustrating search by using TEMPO as the foundation to improving your golf swing. You will have a harmonious blending of techniques forming a smooth, flowing, accurate and powerful swing.

Notes:

TEMPO...

Heartbeat of the Golf Swing

The Little Blue Book I©

By John Michael Saraceno

Golf Educator

Notes:

Realizing the Need

The practice range became my second home because of a neck injury, and a doctor's prescription to take up golf as therapy.

My new challenge was to get the ball to go straight! I used every club in the bag. When using the driver, the ball would slice to the right so badly that I thought it was a boomerang heading back to the tee! Many times while practicing, the resident pros would walk by and say to me, "You need TEMPO!" On the golf course other players would say this also. The message finally got through…I needed TEMPO.

The two questions that needed to be addressed were, "What is TEMPO and how can TEMPO be achieved?" Some said it was timing and others said it was rhythm. No one had an answer except one person who said it would probably take hitting a million golf balls to find it. The calculations revealed that I would have to hit 137 golf balls every day for the next 20 years.

At age 40 I didn't have the time, energy, and money necessary to devote to that project.

There had to be a better way!

As fortune would have it, there was a better way! I found a formula for TEMPO without hitting a million golf balls!

Notes:

Formula Found

TEMPO is necessary for a smooth, flowing and powerful swing desired by players of every level. My question still remained, "How can I achieve TEMPO?" So far, no one could help me with a formula that could be easily applied. One day while on the golf course, I met an "old timer". We walked, talked and played. He mentioned that he had a method for TEMPO. My ears perked up! This was exactly what I was looking for.

As we played he explained that his technique utilized four beats and was applied in the following manner…He started with his left hand on the club, set the club behind the ball and said the word ONE. Then he placed his right hand on the club and said the word TWO. Next, he would take the club away from the golf ball to the height of his backswing saying the word THREE. As he started his downswing, and impacted the ball, he said the word **FOUR.** When he spoke the words ONE, TWO, THREE, they were at his normal speaking tone of voice while the tone for the word **FOUR** was louder.

The beats were not even and steady in terms of tone and interval. He said this four beat method was like four beats in music. Whenever he utilized this method, I noticed the flight of his ball always faded. (That's a ball that tails to the right for right handed players and to the left for left handed players).

Notes:

Formula Found

The same was true for the flight of my golf balls. Something needed adjusting, so I decided to try to develop my own formula.

My first instinct was to choose a TARGET. Then I selected a club for the shot type, placed two hands on the club, set the club behind the ball, and then looked back at the TARGET. LOOKING AT THE TARGET became my first variation for beat ONE.

My karate training taught me to focus beyond the board that I was planning to break. That led me to look at the front side of the golf ball so that I would go beyond the ball. LOOKING AT THE FRONT SIDE OF THE GOLF BALL became the second variation forming beat TWO.

The "old timer's" backswing for beat THREE and his louder beat **FOUR,** impacting the golf ball, was retained.

While working to incorporate these variations, the flight of the ball started on-line to the target but this lasted for only a moment. When the ball reached its maximum height, it slightly faded from the target. Something was still missing…so back to the range.

Notes:

Formula Found

One day while on the range working on my formula and hoping for a breakthrough, a gentleman in the next stall overheard me counting my beats and asked what I was counting. I explained that it was a four beat method for TEMPO and the beats were like four beats in music. He replied that he was a drummer in a Rock 'n' Roll Band and in music the beats should be even and steady…1, 2, 3, 4.

When applying an even and steady four beats, I realized that the beat from three to four was longer, thus establishing a finish at the TARGET. What a revelation! This was the missing link and my final variation. Beat FOUR became a finish at the TARGET. This variation was the final ingredient needed to establish my new formula for TEMPO!

When I put it all together, the formula for TEMPO was to choose a TARGET, place two hands on the club, and set the club behind the ball. ONE was looking at the TARGET. TWO was looking at the FRONT SIDE OF THE GOLF BALL. THREE was the height of the backswing. FOUR was a finish back to the original target…1, 2, 3, 4, with each number beat occurring at a one second interval. With this formula I could easily and consistently apply TEMPO to my swing.

When I applied this formula, the ball flight started out for the TARGET, stayed on-line and landed where it was intended…at the TARGET!! SUCCESS!! Now I knew I wouldn't have to hit a million golf balls to find TEMPO! Neither will you!

Notes:

Joining the Nuts And Bolts

We have defined the formula for TEMPO. Now it is time to join the nuts and bolts. The best way to apply this formula is by VOCALIZING the numbers in a normal speaking tone of voice and associating them with specific points.

ONE – Look at the Target.

TWO – Look at the Front Side of the golf ball.

THREE – Go to the Height of your Backswing. .

FOUR – Finish at the Target.

Each beat is occurring at ONE SECOND INTERVALS.

1 – Target, 2 – Front of Ball, 3 – Backswing, 4 – Target.

You act as your own metronome.

It's just Click, Click, Click, Click.

Counting four simple numbers may seem easy, although coordinating this with a body motion will take practice.

Notes:

Joining the Nuts And Bolts

Before we look at the points associated with the four beats, it is necessary to understand how breathing affects your swing. Breathing is an essential component of a good swing. CONSCIOUSLY BREATHE OFTEN. This will help you stay calm and relaxed.

When you swing with no air in your lungs, you'll be able to move more fluidly, remain calm, and you will keep lower to the ground which is an aid in minimizing topped balls.

The application is simple…after you have set up to the TARGET, it is very important to inhale deeply and then exhale fully. Look at the TARGET, start your count, and swing with no air in your lungs. Add this to your routine. You'll be glad you did.

This breathing technique can be added to every shot type…full swing, pitching, chipping, bunker shots, rough shots, as well as, putting.

Remember to inhale and exhale…Swing with no air in your lungs.

Next, let's now look at the points associated with the four beats in detail.

Notes:

Joining the Nuts And Bolts

ONE:

ONE is looking at the TARGET. What is a Target? Simply put, it is the place you want the ball to come to rest. You MUST have a TARGET before you do anything!! Ray Floyd said that he picks a tree, a branch on that tree, and a leaf on that branch for a Target. You must be that specific when you pick your Target.

After deciding on your TARGET, select a club for the type of shot. Place two hands on the club, and set the club behind the ball. Remember, One is looking at the TARGET.

When you focus on the TARGET, you will produce a swing that will deliver the ball to that TARGET. Many players, when they look at the golf ball, mentally lose focus of the TARGET. Their attention shifts to the golf ball which results in a swing that ends at the golf ball. Their swings are very short and weak, and result in inaccurate shots.

Players, who hold the thought of the TARGET and swing to it, have long swings. Their swings are powerful, and result in accurate shots. Golf is the only "TARGET GAME" that does not give you the opportunity of looking at the TARGET. Therefore, you must keep a mental picture of the TARGET while looking at the golf ball.

Notes:

Joining the Nuts And Bolts

ONE: Looking at the Target.

Notes:

Joining the Nuts And Bolts

TWO:

Many people look at the back side of the golf ball or the top. Still others look at the left or right side. We must be very clear on this point. Contrary to popular belief, you MUST LOOK AT THE GOLF BALL FROM THE FRONT SIDE - that is, the side of the ball FACING THE TARGET.

Why? There are many reasons for this. Most importantly, you will keep centered and not shift too much weight away from the TARGET, thus making your backswing too long. You will be able to shift weight back to the TARGET much quicker and keep your one second interval which will produce more power. Those who tend to sway will now start to rotate their hips. You will gain a larger shoulder turn, producing accurate shots. You will not hit fat shots (shots where the club hits the ground before the ball).

To incorporate this technique, mark the ball with a permanent marker just slightly above the equator of the front side. You will now have a visual point. Later, work using a ball without the mark.

Remember…look at the front side of the golf ball. Train to assimilate this. You'll be glad you did.

Notes:

Joining the Nuts And Bolts

Notes:

Joining the Nuts And Bolts

TWO: Looking at the Front Side of the Golf Ball.

Notes:

Joining the Nuts And Bolts

THREE:

THREE is the HEIGHT OF YOUR BACK SWING. YOU SHOULD STILL BE ABLE TO SEE THE FRONT OF THE BALL WHEN YOU REACH THIS POINT.

In this phase of the golf swing, it is important that when you vocalize the word THREE, it is with only two EE's. If you say the word THREE as THREEEEEE, you have made your backswing too long. You will shift too much weight away from the TARGET, and delay your rotation back to the TARGET. The interval from TWO to THREE is ONE SECOND.

Exceeding this interval is the cause of many errors. The modern swing techniques are geared for a shortened backswing and an elongated forward part of the swing. This creates long, accurate, and powerful swings.

Do not lose sight of the FRONT SIDE OF THE GOLF BALL. Keep a steady ONE SECOND BEAT at THREE and vocalize the word THREE with two EE's only.

Notes:

Joining the Nuts And Bolts

<u>THREE:</u> The Height of the Back Swing.

Notes:

Joining the Nuts And Bolts

FOUR:

Four is a full finish at the TARGET. You should be looking at the FRONT SIDE OF THE GOLF BALL and see the club impact the ball as you finish at the TARGET. That is, the club must move from the height of your backswing at THREE, and make a complete range of motion, finishing with the intention of getting the ball to the TARGET. Contrary to popular belief, FOUR is NOT swinging the club at the golf ball. It is a swing that is BACK TO YOUR ORGINAL TARGET.

Many people simply have a desire for the ball to just go straight. There are 360 degrees of straight. This is not a specific TARGET. If you swing the club with "just going straight" as a goal, you are, in essence, saying that a ball going anywhere is acceptable.

Your mental focus MUST be at the TARGET! So while you are looking at the front side of the ball, you MUST keep the TARGET in your mind, and image that TARGET while swinging. This will avoid short swings that only go to the golf ball, versus long swings that go to the TARGET.

You have a one second interval from THREE to FOUR. There is no half beat at the golf ball. The body motion from THREE to FOUR is one move, similar to an under handed throw of a ball.

Notes:

Joining the Nuts And Bolts

Finishing with the TARGET as your Primary Motivator will produce one of the major techniques all golfers seek…that is, a FOLLOW THROUGH…WHICH WILL BE PART OF YOUR SWING, AND NOT AN ADDED MOTION.

Remember, you are starting with a TARGET and ending with a TARGET. Always keep this in mind.

Notes:

Joining the Nuts And Bolts

FOUR: Finish at the Target.

Notes:

Joining the Nuts And Bolts

Golfers are often too concerned with the mechanical aspects involved in the golf swing. Although they are important, they must be timed properly with good TEMPO.

TEMPO drives these techniques. A good analogy is the engine of a well made automobile, which will perform properly if the fuel and air mixture are fired at the proper time. With proper timing, the engine will perform smoothly, producing the maximum power possible. The same is true for your swing. You may understand the necessary components and perform them mechanically, but unless they are timed properly, they will be unconnected, move around indiscriminately, and produce weak and inaccurate shots.

Remember…BREATHE…count four even steady beats at one second intervals.

ONE - TARGET
TWO - BALL
THREE - BACKSWING
FOUR - TARGET

This is the “Heartbeat” that will keep your swing “Alive”.

This formula is definitive. You will be able to identify and correct your own errors. Just think how much more fun you’ll have and the confidence you will gain in your swing. Now you have a chance to succeed! It’s as simple as 1,2,3,4!

Notes:

Think Inside the Box

When you think inside the box, you will gain the TEMPO for a smooth, effortless swing. The box is defined as the four beats and the associated points, TARGET, BALL, BACKSWING, TARGET - 1, 2, 3, 4, - which occur at one second intervals.

As you vocalize these four even beats in your normal speaking tone of voice, the verbalization will tip you off to where you may be speeding up, slowing down, or being too soft or strong in your tones. You will be able to hear and identify your errors and know where you need to make corrections. The closer you are to maintaining this formula, the closer your shots will be to the TARGET.

Before you actually swing a club, just say the four beats and listen to yourself say the numbers. Listen to your tones, and check the intervals to be sure you are getting to each point…target…ball…back swing…target…all at one second intervals. Mentally, associate each number to one of these points during your actual swing.

Notes:

Think Inside the Box

REMEMBER - THINK INSIDE THE BOX!

BREATHE – SWING WITH LUNGS EMPTY OF AIR

ONE: TARGET

TWO: FRONT SIDE OF BALL

THREE: BACKSWING

FOUR: TARGET

EACH BEAT SHOULD OCCUR AT A ONE SECOND INTERVAL.

Notes:

Champions Are Trained Not Born

Understanding the formula may seem easy. That's great! A good test will be your ability to perform the Walking the Line Drills. When you can perform them with ease, you'll have the foundation for the practical application of TEMPO. This practical application will prepare you for the golf course. To be prepared for the course, PRACTICE is ESSENTIAL.

Walking the Line Drill: Three Ball Drill   

Drills will help you set the foundation necessary for the practical application of TEMPO. The Three Ball Drill can be used anywhere…outdoors or indoors…using any club. This drill will enable you to perform any shot in golf (putting, chipping, pitching, bunker shots, rough shots and full swing with either woods or irons).

On the range when confined by partitions, you may be limited to certain clubs. I suggest you start with a nine iron, and use a chip shot to slowly gain synchronization. As you gain proficiency, move to a pitch shot, then a full swing, and slowly increase the length of the clubs.

This Three Ball Drill is simple. There are three sets each containing three balls. Set up the three balls of each set in a line with an iron club head space between them.

Notes:

THREE BALL DRILL

Notes:

Champions Are Trained Not Born

Pick a target and a club appropriate for the type of shot. The goal here is to be sure you are vocalizing your four beats. Remember …inhale and exhale fully. Then … ONE is the TARGET, TWO is the FRONT SIDE OF THE GOLF BALL, THREE is the height of the BACKSWING, FOUR is back to the original TARGET. These beats should all occur in one second intervals while you are swinging the club. Continue through the drill until you have completed all three balls even if you make a mistake. The idea here is to create a flowing, rhythmic swing.

After you place your hands firmly on the club and set the club behind the golf ball, BREATHE. Inhale when you set up and then exhale before you start your count. Your swing will be completed with no air in your lungs.

Look at and focus on your TARGET and say ONE.

Then LOOK AT THE FRONT SIDE OF THE GOLF BALL and say TWO.

While looking at TWO, take the club away to the HEIGHT OF YOUR BACK SWING and say THREE.

Continue to LOOK AT TWO, THE FRONT SIDE OF THE GOLF BALL, as you start your downswing.

Then take the ball through to the finish at the TARGET, and say FOUR. Remember, you have a one second beat at each point.

Notes:

Champions Are Trained Not Born

Listen to your verbalization of the four beats as you swing the club while working with the first ball. Then just walk up to the second and third ball and repeat this sequence. This is the first set of a three ball set. Complete all three sets WITHOUT STOPPING, except to set up the balls.

Don't get nervous or try to perform these drills perfectly. In the beginning, you will probably make some mistakes. Even if you do, just forget it and keep on going. Be patient. You are practicing to be able to perform a smooth, rhythmic swing motion. Do this often enough and it will become AUTOMATIC!

You can use this drill as a warm-up before you start your practice session. This drill can also be used in the middle or the end of your session as reinforcement and cool down.

Notes:

Champions Are Trained Not Born

THREE BALL DRILL

Notes:

Champions Are Trained Not Born

Walking the Line Drill: Ten Ball Drill

You should use this drill in open spaces, where you can set up a line of ten balls. This drill can be conducted with balls on the grass or on tees. Set the ten balls up just as you did for the Three Ball Drill, with one iron club head space between balls. Start with a nine iron, and work your way up to the driver.

Just as you did in the Three Ball Drill, determine your TARGET and shot type. Remember to BREATHE…inhale, exhale. Look at your target and then start the count. Swing with no air in your lungs. Continue to breathe between shots.

ONE, TWO, THREE, FOUR.

TARGET, BALL, BACKSWING, TARGET.

Listen to your verbalization of the beats while swinging the club for all ten balls. Continue "walking the line." DO NOT STOP even if you make a mistake. Concentrate…just keep on trying to make each tone as close as you can to your normal speaking voice and at one second intervals.

Notes:

Champions Are Trained Not Born

To enhance your skills, challenge yourself. Do two sets of the Ten Ball Drill. When you can complete this with good TEMPO, you can start to wean yourself off the vocalization. Keep the beats in your mind while completing all ten balls. Continue until you can complete them with good TEMPO.

To advance further, continue with the Ten Ball Drill **without** counting mentally, until you can get all ten balls with good TEMPO. At this level, I call this drill the Swing and Go Drill. When you can accomplish the Swing and Go Drill with ten good shots, you are now what I would call a "Machine". Congratulations!!

There will be times when you will lose focus of your TEMPO. This may occur on the practice tee or on the golf course. On the practice tees simply revert to either vocalization or mentally counting your four beats while taking a practice swing. Once you regain your focus you can resume your training without counting.

On the golf course always take a practice swing. You can check your TEMPO by either vocalizing or mentally counting your beats until you regain focus. Then set up and make your swing.

Notes:

Champions Are Trained Not Born

TEN BALL DRILL

Notes:

Champions Are Trained Not Born

TEMPO is the ROCK on which you can base any golf shot. This includes putting, chipping, pitching, bunker shots, rough shots, as well a full swing of woods and irons. You can conduct these drills indoors, on the carpet, or outdoors on the practice area. Utilizing these drills will substantially drop your scores.

Periodically, insert these drills in your practice sessions. Everything learned must be re-enforced regularly. Keep practicing these drills for your on-going education. They will keep you sharp! After twenty years of teaching, I continually add the three ball drill to all my practice sessions.

Notes:

Champions Are Trained Not Born

It is common knowledge among golf instructors that for every swing change you make, it requires 30 days of practice to incorporate it. Be patient while practicing, and be happy with every improvement - no matter how big or how small. Golf is a game for a lifetime. You have plenty of time. Slowly build your foundation, and your swing will be strong and fluid, even when the pressure is on.

When you make the transition from the practice range to the golf course, be sure you are focused on your TARGET. Do not feel self-conscious if you have to verbalize the beats. You can whisper. No one will ever hear you. If they do, does it matter? You are working to perfect your on-course application of TEMPO, and that's all that counts.

Have confidence! You know you can do it! You already have on the practice range! Continue to be focused – stay with your TARGET – BREATHE – and keep a constant firm, not tight, placement of both hands on the club.

Remember, you're playing and practicing to improve, not to be perfect. Getting the ball to the TARGET is all that counts. Assimilating this four beat formula is by far the fastest method to apply TEMPO to all your swing techniques. Let me assure you, you can form a smooth, flowing, accurate and powerful swing!

Notes:

Epilogue

It is my sincere wish that this "Little Blue Book I" takes you to "A New Vista". This formula is the blueprint for adding TEMPO to your golf swing. Juniors like nine year old Ben, who trained with me for five years, championed the use of this formula and shot par. Currently, all my students are utilizing this formula for TEMPO, and are having success. Aspiring professionals and teaching professionals are also using this formula for TEMPO. It is the ROCK on which they have built their swings and the swings of their students. Now you have the opportunity to set the foundation to build your swing!

Techniques described in this book will seem contrary or even outrageous. I believe this is the easiest method to apply TEMPO to your golf swing. It will take practice, patience and perseverance to develop. Please give it a fair chance.

In a recent interview, Ernie Els said that his techniques have not been the best, but that it has been his smooth TEMPO that has enabled him to win tournaments. If TEMPO is the ROCK on which Ernie Els has built his swing, it will most certainly help you! In my twenty years of teaching, I've found that TEMPO is the only constant in the game. It is the ROCK! It works, and is as easy as 1, 2, 3, 4!!

Here's wishing you all the best with your golf game!

John Michael Saraceno
Golf Educator

Notes:

Testimonials

"I was completely frustrated, and had given up on golf. John's 1,2,3,4, tempo method gave me a game. Friends and fellow golfers were astounded at how quickly and consistently I improved. To this day, I use the 1,2,3,4, tempo method for EVERY shot".
Erika Bianchi, Educator, Tech Editor, Student

"John's TEMPO method is easily understood and can be applied by juniors as well as adults".
Terry Felty, PGA, Owner Big Sticks Golf Academy

"This book provides a solution for so many of us who complicate the game by trying to apply all the acquired tips, training and teaching about playing golf". John's solution is as easy as 1,2,3,4!"
Dr. David Marini, Chiropractor, Drummer, Golfer

"I am more fortunate then most because you taught me about "TEMPO" many years ago and I use it with every golf swing. Those that read this book and apply the gift of tempo will see their golf game improve dramatically". Thanks for all the golf lessons".
Robert Saraceno, Businessman, Brother, Golfer.

Notes:

Testimonials

"John's book is a real enhancement to the PGA courses in the PGM program. After reading it, I went out to play a few holes and just focused on counting out the tempo. Lots of good stuff in there!"
Steve Caruso, Bishop Fenwick Graduate, Coastal Carolina U. and PGM student

"A quality book pro…you did a really nice job putting it together - simple, creative, easy to read and put to use. I like how it directs the golfer to immediate improvement on the golf course. Keep up the excellent strides in growing as a golf educator…Bravo!"
Jerry King, Director, Guest Relations, PGA Director of Instruction, Kapalua Land Co. Ltd.

"My last round was an 88. I read John's book and shot an 82. I read it 2 more times to be sure I didn't miss anything and shot 76…Amazing!"
Yat Voong, Businessman, Golfer

Notes:

Testimonials

"I was stuck in a golfers' nightmare! I was always practicing, but never scoring. Then I met John, and his Tempo 1,2,3,4 method. My goal was to be able to score and win against the other players in my foursome…Goal accomplished! I am a firm believer in his system, and until someone proves him wrong, you will find me counting to myself on a course near you! Thank you John!
Allan D. Broome, Operations Manger Harvard University, Golfer and Student

"At age 45 I decided to take up golf. The first time I hit a golf ball I was hooked on the game. I learned to hit the ball with brute strength and little technique that is until I met John the "Swing Guru". John's methodology and belief in tempo as a foundation of a solid swing has turned this 53 year old into a pretty good player. My rounds are now in the low 80's and an occasional round in the 70's. Today I have a solid foundation to fall back on, 1 target) 2 front of ball) 3 top of back swing) 4 back to the target). Thank you John you are the best!"
Bruce Hagopian, Business Owner, Golfer and Student

Notes:

Acknowledgements

God…Thank you for many blessings, too numerous to be mentioned here.

To my Editor…Beverly Kramer…a very special lady. Thank you for your patience, guidance, hard work, and dedication to completing this project. I could not have put this book together without you!

To my Technical Editor…Erika Bianchi…a very special lady and student. Thank you for your assistance and patience in verifying the content and the computer arrangement. Your successes on the course are a "show case" for the TEMPO formula.

To my Chiropractic Crew…Dr. McKiernan, Dr. Marchese, Dr. Marini and Dr. Girardi… Thank you for your care, encouragement and support.

To the "Old Timer"…Thank you for the starting point to develop my own formula for TEMPO.

To my Rock 'n' Roll drummer…Your music lesson was the missing link to finalize my formula for TEMPO.

To my Photographer…John Petrino…the photos are great…the laughs - exceptional.

To all the professionals I've met…Your input was invaluable.

Notes:

Acknowledgements

To my Compliance Editor…Daniel Lagomarsino…Thank you for the design of the back cover. A special thanks for preparing the book for release to the internet. You made it easy for me.

To all my students…You gave me the opportunity to perfect my teaching techniques.

To a very special student…Ben, his father and mother…What a team we made! Ben championed Tempo. His win in the Boston Tour finale of the US Kids Players Championship will never be erased from my mind. I had the pleasure of caddying for this nine year old boy. As we walked to the first tee, I stopped, looked Ben in the eye and said, "Ben, all you have to do today is stay focused on your TARGET and keep your TEMPO. I'll carry the bag. I'll carry you if I have to. The rest is a walk in the park." That's exactly what he did. On a rain soaked course, he shot a score of 72 to par the course winning by 5 strokes.

As Ben and I departed the Putterham Meadow Clubhouse, we noticed a bronze statue of Francis Ouimet and Eddy Lowery, commemorating their US Open win. It's hard to describe what Ben and I experienced as we looked at the statue. I could feel a force emanating from it!

As we looked at each other, we smiled, slapped each other a high five, and both yelled, "WE WON!" I couldn't help feeling that we, too, had added our names to a part of golf history. What a Great Day!

Notes:

Contact the Author

You now have the “Blue Book” that will lift your golf game to a new level.

Thank you for reading “TEMPO…Heartbeat of the Golf Swing”.

We all learn in different ways, and assimilate information at different speeds. I’ve tried to keep things as simple as possible and present information in numerous ways to make it easy to understand. If after having read this book, you require additional clarification, or have any comments or suggestions with regard to the information contained in “The Little Blue Book I”, please feel free to contact me.

Additional Little Blue Books are in the making.
Look for The Little Blue Book II which will address how to establish a precision set-up and The Little Blue Book III which will address how to create mental focus by establishing an overall shot routine.

John Michael Saraceno
Golf Educator

E-mail: TeeItHighLetItFly@Gmail.com

Notes:

About the Author

My entrance into the golf world was the result of a sneeze. Yes, a sneeze causing three vertebrae in my neck to misalign and leaving me with minimal strength in my left arm.

After a week of pain and no sleep, a friend recommended Dr. McKiernan, a Chiropractor. The good doctor helped me with extensive therapy for over a year. He then prescribed exercise, and my taking up golf to strengthen my left arm.

I visited the practice range five days a week, purchasing five jumbo buckets of balls per visit, (120 balls per jumbo bucket). Because my bank account was rapidly depleting, I decided to set up a mini practice range in my living room, with four carpets stacked on the floor, and one folded in half just off the wall. No plastic balls here! I hit the real thing!!! Fortunately, my neighbors never complained and I was able to launch my new career.

During the next twenty years, my career progressed from off-course pro shops to on-course golf shops and then on to resort and private golf clubs.

The teaching phase of my career has evolved from an extensive array of educational programs at various adult education centers as well as various colleges.

Notes:

About the Author

I have intensified my training techniques by utilizing computer aided instruction systems that include the A-Star Video, ModelGolf Digital Video, and the About Golf Simulator.

My current work is almost exclusively with Junior Golf. An assignment with Boston's Inner City Golf Program established by Mayor Menino was my first junior program.

Students are now competing at their respective private courses…The PGA Junior Tour and the USKids Tour.

I am proud to be working as Lead Instructor for the Massachusetts Golf Association and with their new expansion of The First Tee Program.

One of my junior clients competed and won many USKids golf tournaments. He won the USKids Boston Tour Players Championship by shooting par. He qualified for the USKids World Championships held in Pinehurst, North Carolina.

Another shining star is one of my high school team and PGA Junior Tour players who is currently in the PGA Professional Golf Management Program at Coastal Carolina University.

I am now working with a new group of junior golf stars.
The future looks very bright!

Notes:

About the Author

In this most recent phase of my career, I am excited to have had the opportunity to write this book. Life is Good!!

John Michael Saraceno
Golf Educator

Notes:

Made in the USA
Charleston, SC
01 May 2012